The Solar System

Om KIDZ
An imprint of Om Books International

Om Kidz | Om Books International

Reprinted in 2024

Corporate & Editorial Office
A-12, Sector 64, Noida 201 301
Uttar Pradesh, India
Phone: +91 120 477 4100
Email: editorial@ombooks.com
Website: www.ombooksinternational.com

Sales Office
107, Ansari Road, Darya Ganj
New Delhi 110 002, India
Phone: +91 11 4000 9000
Email: sales@ombooks.com
Website: www.ombooks.com

ISBN: 978-93-52765-09-6

Printed in India

10 9 8 7 6 5 4 3 2

Contents

SKY

"Michael, please read this story to me. It is called *The Sky is Falling*. Is the sky really falling?" asked Nancy, anxiously.

"No, Nancy," said Michael, taking the book from her. "The sky is not falling."

"Michael, what is the sky and what is it made of?" asked Nancy.

"The sky is a vast space above the surface of the Earth. It looks like a dome and the atmosphere is an important part," said Michael.

"What is atmosphere?" asked Nancy.

Michael drew a picture and explained, “The atmosphere is a layer of gases that surrounds the Earth. 78% of the Earth’s atmosphere is nitrogen and 21% is oxygen. There are other gases but they are present in much smaller quantities.

“The Earth’s atmosphere has five layers—Troposphere, Stratosphere, Mesosphere, Thermosphere and Exosphere. Each layer is important. As we go higher, the air gets thinner and thinner.”

They looked at the pictures in the book and then at the sky outside.

“So, where does the sky end?” asked Nancy.

“The layers extend more than 1000 km from the surface of the Earth,” Michael replied.

Nancy wondered how long she would take to reach the end of the last layer.

"Do you know why the sky changes colour and becomes dark at night?" asked Michael.

"Is it dark because the Earth is not facing the Sun at night?" Nancy asked.

"That's right! Let me first explain why the sky changes colour. Sunlight is actually a combination of the colours of a rainbow. However, the sky usually appears blue because molecules of air scatter the blue more than the other colours.

"The sky becomes dark at night because at night, the part of the Earth we are on, doesn't face the Sun," Michael replied.

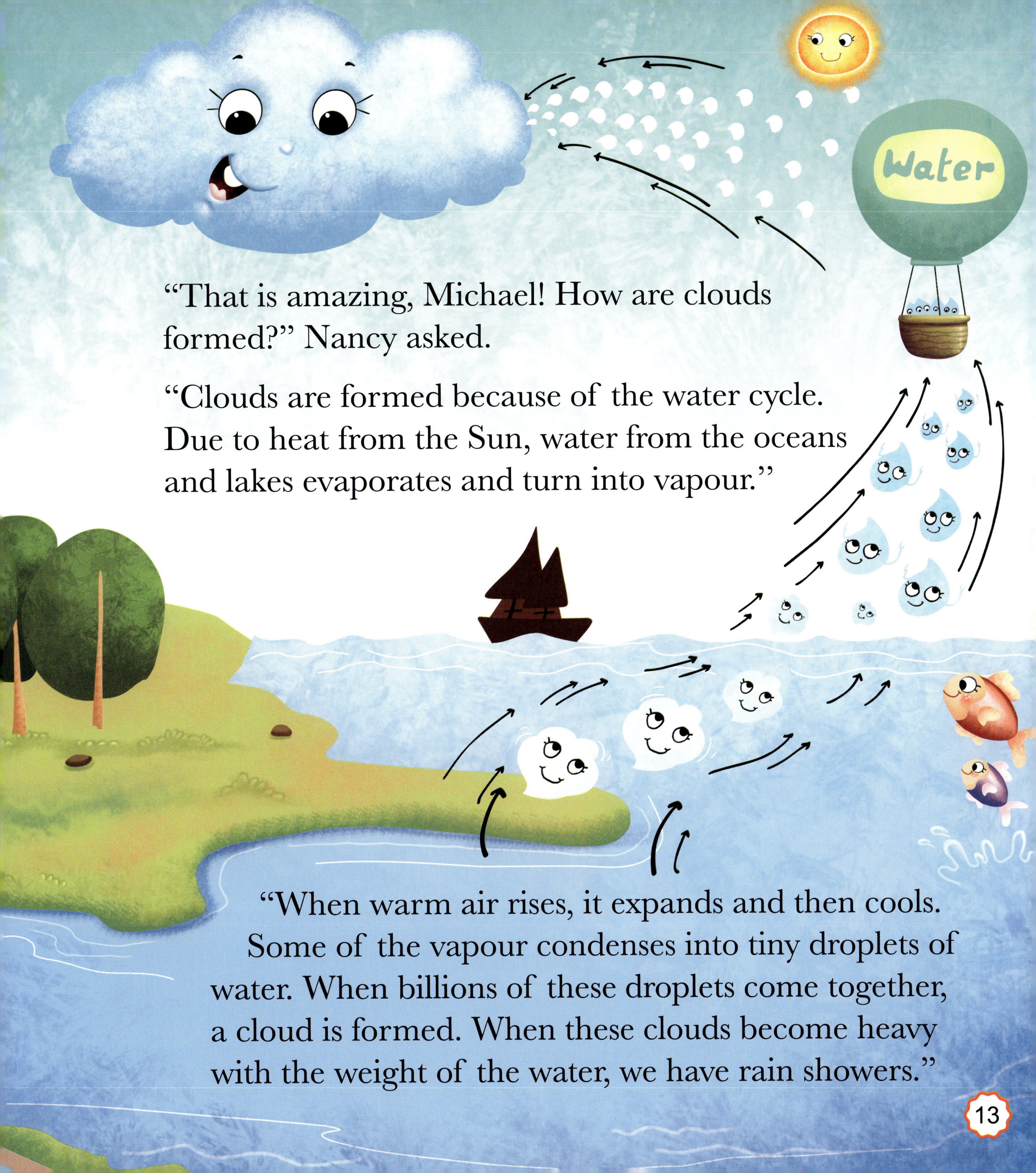

"That is amazing, Michael! How are clouds formed?" Nancy asked.

"Clouds are formed because of the water cycle. Due to heat from the Sun, water from the oceans and lakes evaporates and turn into vapour."

"When warm air rises, it expands and then cools. Some of the vapour condenses into tiny droplets of water. When billions of these droplets come together, a cloud is formed. When these clouds become heavy with the weight of the water, we have rain showers."

“Michael, does the sky look the same from all the planets?” Nancy asked.

“No, Nancy. On most planets, the sky would look dark because there is no atmosphere to scatter the sunlight.”

"I can see the sky meet the Earth's surface. Where do they actually meet?" asked Nancy.

"They do not meet at all! The line at which the Earth's surface and the sky appear to meet is called the horizon," smiled Michael.

"Michael, why doesn't the sky fall down?"

"The sky cannot fall down, Nancy, as it is a mixture of gases. Only rain or snow falls from the sky."
"I want to explore the sky," said Nancy.

The children then spent the rest of the daydreaming about hot air balloon rides.

THE SUN

It was a hot summer day. The sun was shining brightly in the sky.

Mike looked outside and decided that he wanted to play football.

“Sophia, can I go out and play?” asked Mike.

“No Mike, it is very hot outside,” replied Sophia.

“I do not like the Sun. It is so hot. I wish it were night all the time. I love the moonlight and the stars,” said Mike.

"But Mike, the Sun is also a star," said Sophia.

"Then why does it come out during the day?" asked Mike, puzzled.

"The Sun does not come out or move. The Sun is a very large star at the centre of the solar system. All the planets revolve around the Sun in a fixed path called the orbit," said Sophia.

"How is that possible?" wondered Mike.

"It's because the Sun has a very strong gravitational force. This keeps the planets in their orbits," explained Sophia.

"Now I understand. The Sun is important because it keeps the Earth on a fixed path," nodded Mike.

"The Sun is also important because it is the main source of heat and light on the Earth. Without the Sun, the Earth would be a cold and dark place. There would be no life," said Sophia.

“Is the Sun very far away from us?” asked Mike.

“Yes. It is about 150 million kilometres away from the Earth,” replied Sophia.

“Sophia, how does sunlight reach us if the Sun is so far away?”

“Light can travel in space. Even though the Sun is far away, it takes only around 8 minutes for sunlight to reach the Earth,” said Sophia.

"When sunlight reaches the Earth, some of it is absorbed by the Earth's atmosphere and some of it is reflected back into space," she added.

"This maintains a temperature balance on the Earth," explained Sophia.

“Sophia, why would the Earth be lifeless without the Sun?” enquired Mike.

“Plants use sunlight to make food. This process is called photosynthesis. All animals and humans rely on plants for food and oxygen.

Without the Sun, photosynthesis would not be possible and eventually, all life would end," said Sophia.

"Then why does the Sun disappear at night?" asked Mike.

"Mike, the Sun does not disappear. It only seems so because the Earth rotates on its axis," Sophia said. "Let's say that this globe is the Earth and this ball of wool is the Sun," she continued. "When the Earth rotates on its axis, it is daytime for the part of the Earth which faces the Sun. In the other part facing away from the Sun, it is night."

"The Earth also revolves around the Sun as it rotates. This causes the different seasons," Sophia continued.

"Sophia, why does the Sun rise in the East and set in the West?" wondered Mike.

"This is because of the rotation of the Earth.

The Earth rotates to the East, and that's why the Sun appears to rise in the East and move towards the West across the sky," replied Sophia.

"That's wonderful to know! Sophia, it's almost evening. Let's go out and play," Mike said.

"All right, Mike," smiled Sophia.

STARS

Elsa looked at a picture of stars in her book of poems and wondered about them.

She was reciting a poem about stars and decided to ask her brother some questions.

“What are stars? How many stars are there in the sky?” Elsa asked her elder brother, Peter.

“Stars are huge balls of hot gases, mostly hydrogen and helium. There are billions of stars in the universe,” replied Peter.

"How are stars formed?" asked Elsa.

"Stars are formed from giant clouds of helium and hydrogen. When the gases are clumped together, they develop gravity. As gravity increases, dense clouds are formed. They turn into flattened disks, which eventually become stars," said Peter.

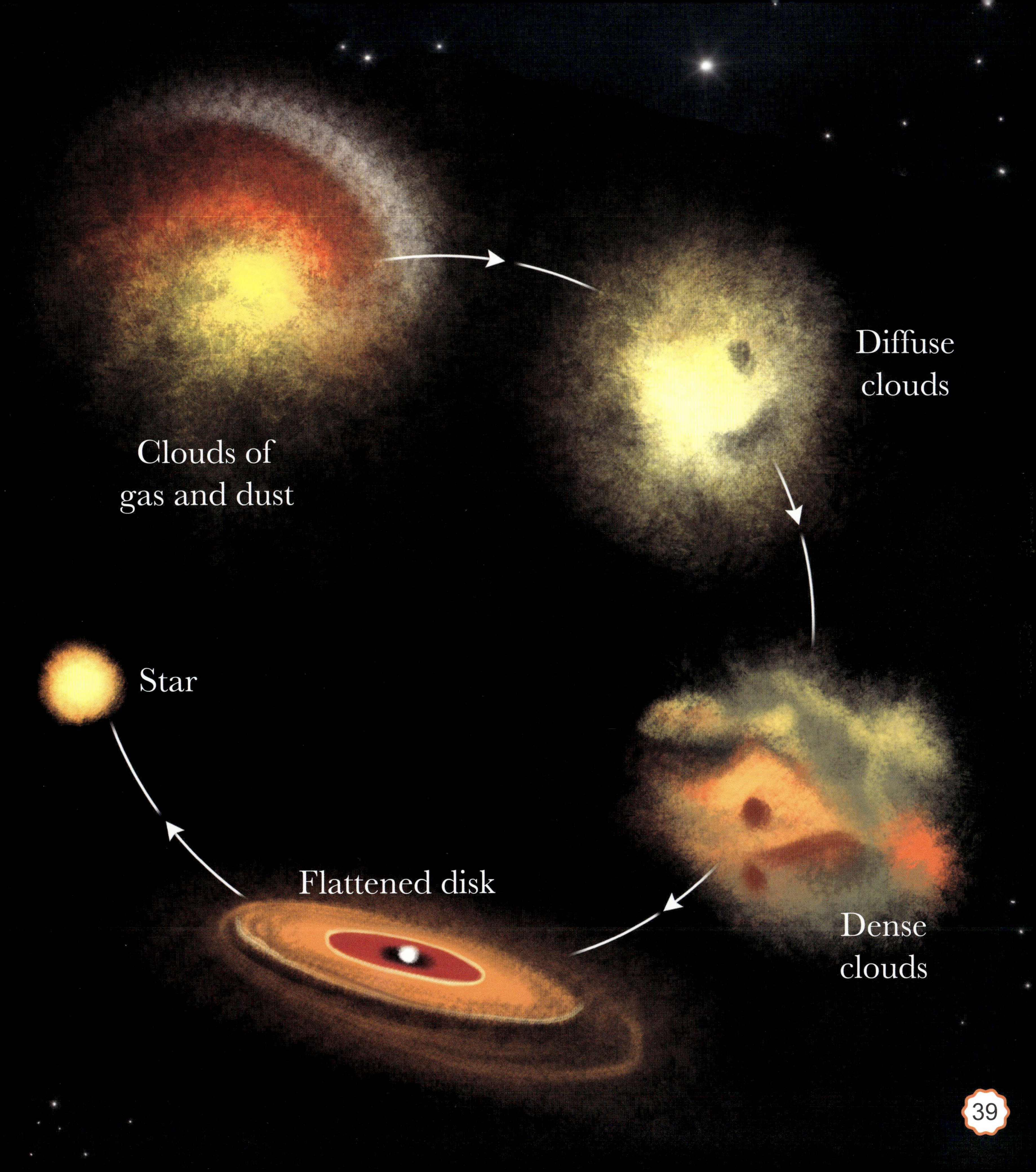
Clouds of
gas and dust
Diffuse
clouds
Dense
clouds
Flattened disk
Star

“Then why do they appear so tiny?” asked Elsa.

“They look so small because they are very far away from the Earth. In fact, the Sun is also a star but it appears so big because it is closer to the Earth,” Peter explained, showing her a poster.

"Does that mean, the small twinkling stars that we see in the sky might be even bigger than the Sun?" Elsa asked, looking at the starry sky from her garden.

"Yes, some stars are bigger than the Sun. But there are also other stars which are smaller," Peter replied.

"In fact, scientists have discovered that stars differ in colour, depending on how hot they are. A star can be blue, green, white, yellow, orange, red or brown. The hottest stars are blue," Peter added.

"Then why do they all look white?" questioned Elsa.

"That is because they are very far away, so our eyes cannot see their actual colour," Peter explained patiently.

"Do stars remain in the universe forever?" asked Elsa.

"No, when the gases that form a star cool down, the star disappears. Also, new stars are being formed all the time. Do you know what a group of stars set in a recognisable pattern is called?" asked Peter, showing her a chart.

"Yes, it is called a constellation," said Elsa.

"That's right, Elsa" smiled Peter.

"Why do stars twinkle?" asked Elsa.

"Stars do not twinkle. When their light enters the Earth, the disturbance in the atmosphere makes them look like they are twinkling," Peter explained.

"Oh! And what are shooting stars?" asked Elsa.

"Shooting stars are actually small pieces of rocks, which burn up on entering the Earth's atmosphere. These rocks are known as meteors," replied Peter.

"Wow, this is so interesting! Now I know everything about stars!" exclaimed Elsa.

"Not everything, Elsa! There is much more to explore when you grow up," said Peter.

PLANETS

"Dad, could you please come here?" Jane called out. She was standing on the terrace with her brother Alex.

"What happened, Jane?" asked Dad.

"Dad, you had told me about the twinkling objects in the sky and explained that they were stars. Now Alex says that the shiny star in the sky is actually a planet called Venus," Jane complained.

"What is a planet?" she asked, as they came down to their father's study.

"Planets are astronomical bodies that move around a star," he explained, showing them a chart. "The Sun is a star. There are eight planets in the solar system which move around the Sun. In order of their distance from the Sun, these planets are Mercury, Venus, Earth, Mars, Jupiter, Saturn, Uranus, and Neptune."

"Are the other planets similar to the Earth? Do people live there, too?" she asked.

"No Jane, the Earth is the only planet which is known to have life. All planets are different from each other. The time they take to revolve around the Sun is also different.

"Mercury completes a revolution around the Sun in about 88 days while Neptune takes more than 60,000 days," Dad explained.

"Dad, please tell me more about the planets," urged Jane.

"Mercury is the smallest planet in the solar system. It is the planet closest to the Sun. Venus is the hottest planet in the solar system. It is known as the Earth's twin because it is similar in size to the Earth. Venus is also the brightest object in the Earth's sky after the Moon. That is why you can see it so clearly."

"But Dad," interrupted Alex, "Why is Venus the hottest planet if Mercury is closest to the Sun?"

"That is because Venus is surrounded by a thick layer of gases which traps all the heat, raising the temperature of the planet," Dad explained.

“Next is Mars, which is also known as the red planet because its surface is covered with reddish-brown soil. It is a cold planet and scientists believe that it has liquid water.”

“After that is Jupiter, the largest planet in the solar system. All the planets of our solar system can fit into it. However, Jupiter has the shortest day. Its day is only around 10-hours long. This is because Jupiter spins very fast on its axis,” Dad explained, showing them models of the planets.

"Saturn looks very beautiful because of the cluster of rings around it. This planet is very light and it would float if dipped in water," said Dad.

"Uranus is a very large and cold planet. Its atmosphere is made up of icy water and gases. Uranus is the only planet that is tilted by almost 98 degrees," he continued.

"Dad, why is Neptune blue?" asked Alex.

"It is blue because of the presence of a gas called methane in its atmosphere. Neptune has six rings around it. It is also a very cold planet because it is far away from the Sun," replied Dad, showing them an image of the planet.

"I would like to become an astronaut when I grow up so that I can visit all these planets," said Jane.

THE MOON

It was late in the evening. Eric was reading a story. When he looked up, he saw the moon through the window. He was puzzled.

"What's the matter, Eric?" asked his sister, Chloe.

"Look at the moon! Have you noticed it has changed its shape?" said Eric.

Eric took Chloe to the terrace.

"Look! The moon was like a full circle a few days ago. Today there is only half of it. Is it disappearing?" asked Eric.

"The moon is not disappearing, Eric," said Chloe. "You are just seeing one of its phases."

"What are phases?" asked Eric.
"Why do they occur?"

"The moon is a celestial body made up of rocks. It goes around the Earth on a fixed path called the orbit. The moon has no light of its own. It shines when the light of the Sun falls on it," said Chloe.

"How does that happen?" wondered Eric.

"The surface of the moon reflects sunlight. Light can pass through only some objects. Look at this wall," said Chloe, pointing towards a torch at the wall. "What do you see?"

"I can see a part of the wall lit up," replied Eric.

"Exactly! The light falling on the wall cannot pass through it and gets reflected. You can see the wall due to this reflected light. In the same way, when the Sun's light falls on the moon, it cannot pass through the moon. It gets reflected. This is the light that makes the moon visible to us," explained Chloe.

"Now I understand, the moon disappears when it doesn't get sunlight!" said Eric.

"No, Eric. As the moon goes around the Earth, it gets sunlight from various angles. This causes the different phases of the moon."

"Suppose this ball is the moon and the torch is the Sun.

When I shine the torch on the ball, you cannot see the lit-up side. You are facing the opposite side which is dark.

When sunlight falls on the side of the moon facing away from the Earth, it is called the New Moon.

"Then, as the moon goes around the Earth, we see more and more of the sunlit side. Finally, when the Earth has the moon on one side and the Sun on the other side, we are able to see a Full Moon," explained Chloe.

"When we look at the moon, it seems like it has a face," said Eric.

"Yes, it seems so. When people say that they can see a face on the moon, what they actually see is the uneven surface of the moon. There are deep holes called craters, and hills on the moon's surface which, when seen from the Earth, look like a face," said Chloe.

“How do we know that the moon has craters and hills?” asked Eric.

“In 1969, astronauts Neil Armstrong, Michael Collins and Buzz Aldrin became the first human beings to fly a spacecraft to the moon. Armstrong was the first to set foot on its surface,” replied Chloe.

"The astronauts explored the surface of the moon and took photographs."

“They also planted an American flag on the moon and collected moon rocks for the scientists to study,” she continued.

After listening to his sister, Eric was relieved to know that the moon was not disappearing.

Now, each time Eric sees the crescent moon, he knows what's happening.

EARTH

Kelly was playing with her toys in the living room. Mom was on the phone talking to Dad. He was in Australia for work. After Mom hung up, Kelly asked her, "What was Dad doing?"

“He was on his way to office,” replied Mom.

“At night?” Kelly asked.

“No Kelly, it is daytime in Australia.”

"How is that possible?" asked Kelly, surprised.

"That is because the Earth is rotating on its axis," said Mom.

"Rotating! How?" Kelly asked.

"The Earth is like this top, rotating on its axis," said Mom, spinning a top on the table.

"If the Earth is rotating, then why don't we feel its movement?" asked Kelly.

"That's because the speed of the Earth is constant," explained Mom. "For example, if you are in a car which is moving at aconstant speed on a smooth surface, you will not feel much movement."

"Okay. But why do different parts of the world have day and night at different times?" asked Kelly.

"The Earth is a part of the solar system. The solar system is made up of the planets, their moons and other smaller bodies like asteroids, meteoroids, and comets," said Mom.

"Now, let us assume that this ball is the Earth and the lamp is the Sun. The Earth rotates on its axis and completes one rotation in about 24 hours, which is one day."

On the side of the Earth facing the Sun, it is daytime and on the side facing away from it, it is night-time. This is why different parts of the world have day and night at different times," said Mom.

"How long does it take for the Earth to complete one revolution around the Sun?" Kelly asked.

"The Earth takes around 365 days to complete one revolution around the Sun. The tilt of the Earth during its revolution causes the different seasons," explained Mom.

"Yes, I know about the four seasons – summer, autumn, winter and spring," replied Kelly.

"Mom, you said that there are more planets in our solar system. Are they similar to the Earth?" enquired Kelly.

"No. The Earth is the only planet where life exists. It is surrounded by a thick layer of gases called atmosphere."

"The atmosphere has many gases, including oxygen, nitrogen and hydrogen. Also, about 71% of the Earth's surface is covered with water."

"This is why plants, animals, humans and other creatures can survive on the Earth," said Mom.

"How large is the Earth, Mom?" asked Kelly.

"The Earth's length from the North Pole to the South Pole is around 40,000 km," Mom replied.

"How do they measure the Earth?" asked Kelly, imagining an astronaut with a huge measuring tape.

"It is measured with the help of mathematical calculations," replied Mom.

"It must be wonderful to see the Earth from space," said Kelly, imagining herself taking a trip around the Earth.